Welcome to The Power of Story

We are delighted that you are here. Your presence with us signals a season of change, a time to dig into the Word and hear God speak as you write your story.

As we launch out into The Power of Story, we begin with a Bible study on a brilliant verse packed with truth from Ephesians chapter two. Starting in the Word guides you to spend time with Jesus, filling your mind and heart with His truth. When you are convinced that He is good and that you are called, you can walk forward fearlessly with FlourishWriters.

We invite you to create a quiet space to cultivate confidence in your life right now. We pray that as you posture yourself to hear, you will receive the Word that you need to step forward into the fulfillment of the promises that God has spoken.

Whatever the circumstances of your life right now, God's Word is waiting to meet you exactly where you are, helping you prepare to write.

We pray that you become *"like an olive tree flourishing in the house of God . . . trusting in God's unfailing love for ever and ever."* Psalm 52:8 (NIV) Our desire is to keep you anchored to His love during this adventure into writing your story.

Prepare to be amazed as you pursue the daily practices of the DECLARE Bible Study Approach. One friend likens it to *"Holy Spirit sunglasses"* that allow you to see through the surface into the deep waters: *"I've been able to see deeper into the Bible than I've ever done before. The Holy Spirit has used DECLARE to bring much more life into my Bible time."*

May the seeds planted in your life grow as you open the Bible and enjoy time in God's presence. We stand with you in expectation at how Jesus is going to show up in your life as you feast on His Word and prepare to write your God Story.

Mindy & Jenny

P.S. Go ahead and watch the Video: Welcome to the Power of Story.

Course Overview

Introduction 1

Let's get everything ready to go! The Introduction helps you prepare for a successful experience by presenting the following tasks:

- Read the Welcome Letter on page 1 (you probably just did).
- Watch the Video: Welcome to the Power of Story.
- Read the Course Overview (you are here!).
- Set goals with the Course Schedule (page 5)
- Watch the Video and Read: How to Get the Most from this Course (pages 6-7).
- Meet Your Instructors (page 8).
- Watch the Video: Tour of the Learning Portal and make motes on page 9.

Getting Started 11

Before we begin the writing process, we spend time in God's Word to confirm our call to write. We use the DECLARE Bible Study Approach and Ephesians 2:10 as our Declaration Verse: "For we are God's handiwork, created in Christ Jesus to do good works, which God prepared in advance for us to do." (NIV)

- Reflect on Ephesians 2:10.
- Confirm God's call for you to write.
- Learn to use the DECLARE Bible Study Approach.

Prayer Guide 29

Staying connected with God through prayer is not just a good idea -- it's a necessity. Open prayer channels help you engage with the Lord as you write. The Prayer Guide provides questions for you to process with God as you create your personal Spiritual Battle Plan.

- Stay close to God during the writing process.
- Fuel your determination through prayer.
- Identify lies that will thwart your success.
- Replace these lies with truth from the Word of God.

© Copyright 2019

by Melinda Kiker & Jennifer Kochert

All rights reserved. This book or any portion thereof may not be reproduced or used in any manner whatsoever without the express written permission of the publisher except for the use of brief quotations in a book review.

Flourish Ministries LLC
FlourishGathering.com

Unless otherwise marked, Scripture quotations are taken from THE HOLY BIBLE, NEW INTERNATIONAL VERSION® NIV® Copyright © 1973, 1978, 1984 by International Bible Society® Used by permission. All rights reserved worldwide

Unless otherwise marked, Scripture quotations marked (NLT) are taken from the Holy Bible, New Living Translation, copyright ©1996, 2004, 2015 by Tyndale House Foundation. Used by permission of Tyndale House Publishers, Inc., Carol Stream, Illinois 60188. All rights reserved.

Unless otherwise marked, Scripture quotations are from The ESV® Bible (The Holy Bible, English Standard Version®), copyright © 2001 by Crossway, a publishing ministry of Good News Publishers. Used by permission. All rights reserved.

Idea Phase 44

What should I write? Moving into the Idea Phase, you further engage with God as you journal, reflect, and listen. You consider many stories that could be told as you explore different possibilities.

- Gather insights from Ephesians 2:10.
- Create a timeline for personal reflection.
- Brainstorm your story ideas.
- Create a Support Team.

Planning Phase 60

What do I include in my story? During the Planning Phase, we zero in on the specific story you are called to write. The step-by-step planning process guides you to summarize your story idea and reflect on your Key Scripture.

- Choose the specific story you are called to write.
- Create a devotional map to plan your story idea.
- Study your Key Scripture.

Organizing Phase 77

How do I prepare to write? Now that you have identified the specific story you're going to write, it's time to get organized. The organizing process guides you to clarify the purpose your story will communicate. The purpose is supported by your Key Scripture which anchors your story in God's Word.

- Refine and summarize the details of your story.
- Write a Purpose Statement.
- Understand the needs of your reader.
- Prepare to write by creating a devotional outline.

Writing Phase 87

How do I complete my first draft? After completing the planning and organizing process, you're prepared to get those words from your head onto paper. Even the most reluctant writer discovers that they are ready to write with the tools provided. The writing process is guided by examples which demonstrate how to create a first draft.

- Practice the craft of a well-written story.
- Learn how to overcome writer's block.
- Discover the elements of the crucial first paragraph.
- Write your first draft.

Editing Phase 100

How do I strengthen my writing? Now that you have a first draft, it's time to get down to the nitty gritty of editing and revision. We want to help you to tighten the prose so that your story connects to your readers. We provide guidelines for a Friend Edit and a handy Self-Edit checklist to overcome the common pitfalls of devotional writers.

- Learn an organized approach to edit and revise the content of your first draft.
- Engage with your support team for a Friend Edit.
- Use the Self-Edit checklist to revise your devotional.
- Polish your writing and choose a title.

Publishing Phase 121

How can I share my story? Sit back in satisfaction with your devotional in your hands. You have created a testimony of the Lord's faithfulness that is ready to shine for His glory. This final phase of the writing process guides you to prayerfully consider how to share your story.

- Follow God's lead as you decide how to share your story.
- Use reader feedback to grow as a writer.
- Seek a FlourishWriters Devotional Review if desired.

Course Schedule

Use the Course Schedule to set goals. Most modules take 1 - 2 weeks to complete. We have found that students finish the course in 8-12 weeks on average:

Introduction *(est. week 1)*

Completion Date: _____

Getting Started *(est. weeks 2-3)*

Completion Date: _____

Prayer Guide *(est. week 4)*

Completion Date: _____

Idea Phase *(est. week 5)*

Completion Date: _____

Planning Phase *(est. weeks6)*

Completion Date: _____

Organizing Phase *(est. week 7)*

Completion Date: _____

Writing Phase *(est. weeks 8-9)*

Completion Date: _____

Editing Phase *(est. weeks 10-11)*

Completion Date: _____

Publishing Phase *(est. week 12)*

Completion Date: _____

Days and times I plan to work on the course:

_____

_____

How to Get the Most from this Course

We want to share with you how to get the most out of FlourishWriters and The Power of Story. Like most things in life, you get out what you put into it. Go the gym and watch others do the heavy lifting, and not much is going to happen to your muscles -- but grab a set of dumbbells, start reaching for the sky, and you'll see results! Embarking on a FlourishWriters training program will strengthen your writing muscles. And now for some hot tips on how to succeed:

1. **Fight for Your Fifteen.** Set aside at least 15 minutes each day or a longer block of time in your week to work through the course content. Please use the **Course Schedule** to create a plan to finish the course in good time. *"Commit to the Lord whatever you do, and he will establish your plans." (Proverbs 15:3)*

2. **Get Curious About the Word.** What does the Word say about you, your story, your past and your future? What does the Word say about God himself? As you spend time in the Bible, listening to God's voice, and reflecting on your story of redemption, you will gain clarity regarding your writing project. The DECLARE Bible Study Approach guides you to spend quality time in the Word.

3. **Stay Close to Jesus.** Jesus is the Word personified. He embodies everything God desires to reveal to us. John tells us *"the Word became flesh and dwelt among us." (John 1:14)* That's Jesus! He is our guide to writing our God Story.

4. **Seek for a Personal Word.** The writing process is a listening process. We desire to follow the Lord's leading and receive His anointing to write. When we pursue God in this way, and the inevitable storms come, the Word that God has spoken will hold us like an anchor to the Rock.

5. **Trust the Process.** The **Course Overview** and **Module Checklists** are designed to keep you on track. We created the course as a step-by-step process. The assignments are not just suggestions, but as you answer the questions and do the work, your confidence and skill will grow. You will do best not to skip around the course. Complete each module content in the order it is presented.

6. **Keep Writing.** If you become stalled out at any part of the course, prayerfully consider where the road block is coming from, seek God, and press through. You may want to go back to your **Prayer Guide** and stand on the promises God spoke. Also, reach out to your Support Team or to your instructors, Jenny and Mindy, at info@flourishgathering.com.

7. **Stay Connected.** Please join us for our monthly coaching calls to engage with us live, ask questions, and grow as a writer. We invite you to comment on the learning portal if you have any questions or comments about the modules. If you're on Facebook, our FlourishWriters group provides lively conversation and help from your instructors and other students:

   https://www.facebook.com/groups/223037428309976/

When you set goals and work consistently toward those, you build the foundation for success. The FlourishWriters Devotional Writing Process guides you to press into God's Word and hear His voice. You gain confidence that He will never fail you.

God may not answer like you imagined, but He desires to lead you forward. One of the characteristics of God is that He loves multiplication. This is good news! **When pursuing God, you get out more than you put into it.** Psalm 34:4 says, *"God met me more than halfway." (MSG)*

We're thrilled that you're here, becoming a FlourishWriter who reveals The Power of Story.

Meet Your Instructors

Mindy

Mindy Kiker is a committed Floridian, enjoying a quiet woodland home that she and her husband built to shelter their four boisterous boys. A favorite verse that motivates her to keep pressing into God and encouraging her friends to do the same is Galatians 5:1, "It is for freedom that Christ has set us free. Stand firm, then, and do not let yourselves be burdened again by a yoke of slavery."

Jenny

Jenny Kochert was born and raised in sunny South Florida. Jenny, her husband Ryan, and daughter Sophia now live in Northern Kentucky where they serve in ministry together as a family. God has put a story on her lips and a passion in her heart to encourage women, and she is thrilled that she gets to do that each and every day.

Tour of the Learning Portal

Watch Video and take notes here:

Getting Started

Getting Started

Welcome to **The Power of Story**.

Before we begin the writing process, we will spend time in God's Word to confirm our call to write. We use the DECLARE Bible Study Approach with Ephesians 2:10 as our Declaration Verse: "For we are God's handiwork, created in Christ Jesus to do good works, which God God prepared in advance for us to do." (NIV)

As you get started, you will:

- Reflect on Ephesians 2:10.
- Confirm God's call for you to write your story.
- Learn to use the DECLARE Bible Study Approach.

Getting Started Checklist

Use this step-by-step checklist to complete the content for this module. It will guide you as you navigate through the workbook and videos included in this module of The Power of Story.

- [ ] Watch the Video: Confirm God's Call to Write

- [ ] Watch the Videos: DECLARE Bible Study Approach, Parts I, II, and III.

- [ ] Read The DECLARE Bible Study Approach overview on Pages 14-15.

- [ ] Read the Devotional: God's Handiwork on Pages 16-18.

- [ ] Complete Workbook Pages 19-27.

DECLARE Bible Study Approach

"We know that the Son of God has come and has given us understanding, so that we may know him who is true...."

1 John 5:20

The **DECLARE Bible Study Approach** equips us to dig deeper into a passage of scripture in order to know God's Word intimately and apply it to our lives. *(1 Corinthians 2:10-15)* When His Word is activated in our midst, new life is released, and we will begin to flourish where we are planted.

Preparation: Engage

Whenever you have time to dig into the Word, it is important to engage by tuning your ears and heart to God's voice. Take just a few minutes to pray through the following items:

Toss: Throw your cares on God. Let Him bear your burdens. *Psalm 55:22*
Catch: Receive the peace that surpasses all understanding. *Philippians 4:7*
Invite: Take every thought captive. Invite clarity and focus. Refuse confusion, distraction, or double-mindedness. *2 Corinthians 10:5*
Open: Ask God if you have turned away or closed your heart to anyone. Release the offense, open your heart, and give the situation into God's care. *Psalm 139:23*
Expect: Tell God that you are looking forward to hearing from Him. Let the excitement of time in His presence build expectation in your heart. *Habakkuk 2:1*

Declare Practice: Read & Write

Start with a verse or short passage that you want to explore further:

- Read the scripture slowly once or twice, even out loud if you are able.
- Write the scripture in your journal, including verses before and after.
- Read the entire chapter for context.
- Read the passage in another translation.

Declare Practice: Investigate

Once you have read the Scripture and corresponding chapter, there are several options that you can use to look deeper into the meditation Scripture. Investigate as little or as much as time allows. Online resources like BibleGateway.com or BlueLetterBible.org will help:
- Highlight the words in the meditation verse you want to research more. Do a word study to gain greater insight into the passage.
- Read correlating verses, also called cross references. Reading cross references will help you better understand a verse, word, or principle.
- Read a commentary.

Declare Practice: Imagine

Read the meditation verse and insert yourself in the story. Use your imagination to be present in the scene. Ask yourself the following questions:

- When and where is this taking place?
- Who is speaking? About what? Why?
- What are the characteristics of God as shown through this Scripture or chapter?
- What are the promises of God as shown through this Scripture or chapter?

Declare Practice: Listen

Invite the Words of Scripture and the Words of God to speak personally into your mind and heart. You can ask these questions:

- How do these verses apply to me?
- Is there anything that I need to receive or surrender in my life?
- Lord, how I can apply your Word to the frustrations, disappointments, fears, or hurts in my life?

Listening can be pursued for several days, and in fact, God will probably speak unexpectedly at random times of day or night as His revelation is released to you.

Declare Practice: Declare

Write out a declaration of what you have received as you meditated on the Word. This can be a statement of God's promise to you, an affirmation of the healing that He has given you, or a proclamation of a truth that has become real to you. A declaration can include Scripture or your own words, or some of each.

Devotional: God's Handiwork

You've most likely heard the phrase, "Beauty is in the eye of the beholder."

What do you think when you hear this statement?

The first thing that comes to mind is that we all "see" things differently. One person may see something beautiful while another may perceive an alternative reality.

Recently, I chatted with my neighbor while overlooking our adjoining backyard. She lamented that the dandelions were overtaking her yard and wanted them gone as soon as possible. As I looked out at my yard, I saw the same dandelions, yet I thought they were rather beautiful. A kaleidoscope of yellow and white with puffs of pink washed over our Kentucky bluegrass, bringing a smile to my face. After a long winter, new life was beginning to flourish, and those dandelions hinted at my hope of warmer days to come.

I wondered how two could people see the same thing, yet one sees something beautiful while the other sees merely a worthless weed? As I pondered this mystery, I remembered Paul's words in Ephesians 2:10:

> "For we are his handiwork, created in Christ Jesus to do good works, which God prepared in advance for us to do." (NIV)

The New Living Translation describes us as God's "masterpiece." What do you think of when you hear the word "masterpiece?" Do you think of valuable, priceless, beautiful?

As I caught glimpses of those dandelions throughout the pockets of my busy day, my eye saw a masterpiece. My eye saw the hope of spring I longed for!

However, I could easily have seen the weeds that dandelions are labeled: ugly and useless, a landscaper's nuisance. Yet, I wonder what God saw when He first created the dandelion?

Every human is marred by the stains of a sin-scorched world. Seasons of our lives are consumed in flames, leaving a heap of dirty ashes. The accuser labels us with derisive words: ugly, useless, a nuisance – anything but beautiful. These labels tangle our hearts with weeds, obscuring the beauty of our garden. And just like the dandelion, we see our life stories as worthless and invaluable. Unfortunately, we cannot take a mower to our ugly stories and make them disappear.

So, what are we to do? How can we see our life and our identity as the masterpieces they are?

In Ephesians 2:10, Paul speaks an affirmation to the Church of Ephesus, calling out their Christ-given destiny. He reminds us that we are God's very best work, His most priceless possession, the pinnacle of beauty simply because we bear His name.

Why are we priceless, beautiful, worthy? Because of Christ Jesus. Because of the price paid for our sin.

In God's rich mercy and great love, He calls us back to Him, back to our original design. He makes us alive in Christ (Ephesians 2:4-5). And because of this we are not merely redeemed and set free from the bondage of sin and death. God personalizes our redemption by calling us His children. He esteems us as His greatest accomplishment. The ugly stories and the labels of shame and worthlessness have all been washed anew.

One of my favorite Scriptures is found in Isaiah 61:3 where God chooses to exchange our grieving hearts and bestow on us a crown of beauty:

> *". . . to bestow on them a crown of beauty instead of ashes,*
> *the oil of joy instead of mourning,*
> *and a garment of praise instead of a spirit of despair.*
> *They will be called oaks of righteousness,*
> *a planting of the LORD for the display of his splendor". (NIV)*

God's Word again and again affirms the truth of who we are. We are God's handiwork, simply because we are worth it! Because we are greatly loved! Because we are His masterpiece!

As if the promises found in Ephesians 2:10 couldn't get any better, God declares that we have been created to do good works that He has already prepared for us to do. Just like the world's greatest artists have created masterpieces to serve their purpose as admirer's revel at their beauty.

We too have been created with a purpose. And our stories -- the ones we deem to be worthless, unsightly weeds in the garden of our lives -- have some of the greatest potential to display God's glory.

Today, I pray that you allow the truths from God's Word to soak into the places of your life that you don't see as beautiful. Invite His light into the stories that you have judged to be worthless or invaluable. Ask God to show you how He sees your stories.

As I gaze fondly at those dandelions in my backyard, I appreciate that they are resilient. They keep coming back, springing forth with new life, fulfilling their purpose, undaunted by how others see them.

Let us cultivate lives that display the majestic splendor of the Master Creator through our stories, standing strong on God's Word as truth.

May you recognize your worth as you walk into your Christ-given inheritance.

DECLARE Stage One: Read & Write

Declaration Verse: Ephesians 2:10

"For we are God's handiwork, created in Christ Jesus to do good works, which God prepared in advance for us to do." Ephesians 2:10 *(NIV)*

[ ] Read Ephesians 2:10 slowly once or twice, even out loud if you are able.

[ ] Write Ephesians 2: 9-11 in the space below. *Feel free to get creative.*

[ ] Read Ephesians chapter 2 for context. Write out a few observations:

[ ] Read Ephesians 2:10 in another Bible translation. Do you notice any differences?

Write your observations:

DECLARE Stage Two: Investigate

Let's look deeper into the Declaration Verse. Investigate as little or as much as time allows. Online resources like BibleGateway.com or BlueLetterBible.org will help you during your investigation.

[ ] Conduct a Word Study: Part One

Read the Declaration Verse or the entire chapter if you have more time. Spend a few minutes identifying any words you want to research.

[ ] Conduct a Word Study: Part Two

Using BlueLetterBible.org or another online resource, choose a word you selected above to conduct your word study. This is as simple as looking up the original Greek or Hebrew word, reading the definitions of that word, and looking at how it is used in other verses in the Bible.

[ ] Read any of the following cross references for Ephesians 2:10. Reading cross references will help you better understand a verse, word, or principle:

> *Isaiah 43:10*
> *Colossians 1: 9-11*
> *2 Corinthians 5:17*

What did you discover? Write your insights:

[ ] Read a commentary. A commentary is a collection of explanatory notes that a Bible scholar has written about passages of scripture. Write any observations, quotes, or notes:

DECLARE Stage Three: Imagine

Remember to take a moment to "Engage" (pg. 14) as you prepare to listen: toss, catch, invite, open, expect. Refer again to the DECLARE video series if needed. Invite the Words of Scripture and the Words of God to speak into your mind and heart.

[ ] Read Ephesians 2:10

You may want to scout around in your Bible for any notes or perhaps an introduction to this book of the Bible. When using your imagination, it helps to keep in mind the context of the chapter and book that you're in. Insert yourself in the story as you ponder the following questions. Use your imagination and all your senses to be present in the scene.

[ ] When and where is this taking place? What do you imagine you might see, hear, touch, taste, or smell?

[ ] Who is speaking or writing? Who are they addressing? Others? God? Themselves?

[ ] What are they speaking or writing about? What is their purpose?

[ ] What are the characteristics of God as shown through the Declaration Verse or chapter? Is He steadfast, faithful, just, trustworthy, nurturing, kind, gentle, or strong? What do you see revealed about His nature in this passage of Scripture?

[ ] What are the promises of God as shown through the Declaration Verse or chapter? Write any observations, key words, or questions you have as you ponder the Declaration Verse. If you have time, you may want to do another word study.

DECLARE Stage Four: Listen

> *Remember to take a moment to "Engage" as you prepare to listen: toss, catch, invite, open, expect. Invite the Words of Scripture and the Words of God to speak personally into your mind and heart. Remember that God's voice will never accuse you. He may bring gentle conviction, and that can cause some grief, but Jesus always brings hope.*

Listening can be pursued for several days, and in fact, God will probably speak unexpectedly at random times of day or night as His revelation is released to you. Ask these questions as you listen to God's voice:

[ ] How does the Declaration Verse apply to me?

[ ] Ponder and pray: how I can apply these truths to the frustrations, disappointments, fears, or hurts in my life? Is there anything I need to surrender or receive in my life.

DECLARE Stage Five: Declare

Declaration Verse: Ephesians 2:10

Write out a declaration of what you have received as you meditated on the Word. This can be a statement of God's promise to you, an affirmation of the healing that He has given you, or a proclamation of a truth that has become real to you. A declaration can include Scripture or your own words, or some of each.

Write out Ephesians 2:10 by hand if you memorized it or summarize the Declaration Verse in your own words below. Spend a few minutes documenting your insights, "a-ha" moments, and revelations from your time of digging into the Bible.

Prayer Guide

Prayer Guide

Staying connected with God through prayer is not just a good idea -- it is a necessity. Open prayer channels help you to engage with the Lord as you write. The Prayer Guide provides questions for you to process with God to create your personal Spiritual Battle Plan.

As you work through the Prayer Guide and create a Spiritual Battle Plan, you will:

- Stay close to God during the writing process.
- Fuel your determination through prayer.
- Identify lies that will thwart your success.
- Replace these lies with truth from the Word of God.

Prayer Guide Checklist

Use this step-by-step checklist to complete the content for this phase. It will guide you as you navigate through the workbook and videos included in this phase of The Power of Story course.

- [ ] Watch the Video: Introduction to the Spiritual Battle Plan

- [ ] Watch the Video: Preparing Your Spiritual Battle Plan

- [ ] Read Workbook Pages 32-36.

- [ ] Prepare Your Personal Battle Plan Pages 38-42.

My Spiritual Battle Plan

In Ephesians chapter 2, verse 5, we see that God rescues us from death by making us alive in Christ. We are saved by His grace. He created us as a masterpiece, a poem, a song that praises His majesty (verse 10).

What a thrilling promise. What hope.

The Master Creator takes great care to fashion each one of us in His image. We are fearfully and wonderfully made (Psalm 139: 14). He designs us with careful thought and imagination (Psalm 40:5). He stands back and marvels at each glorious man and woman and calls us blessed (Genesis 1:27-18).

Listen to the words of the Lord who created you, *"Fear not, for I have redeemed you; I have called you by name, you are mine." Isaiah 43:1 (ESV)*

Selah. Pause and think of that. The God of the universe promises, *"I have called you by name. You are mine."*

By joining FlourishWriters, you have chosen to step out in faith as you write your story of Jehovah God's redemption in your life. In the writing process, you will learn about yourself and about God. You will affirm the Lord's goodness in your own heart, and your story will become a light shining forth to reveal God's redeeming power to others.

Does Satan like this?

Absolutely not.

He will do everything in his power to thwart this revelation. Not to alarm you, **but there is a cosmic battle for your story.** It is a battle that God has already won, but you have to partner with Him to see the victory.

As you draw near to your Provider and Protector, you will see your story as a journey to becoming God's masterpiece described in Ephesians 2:10. Satan is eager to twist or taint your story, to focus your memories on the pain, the loss, and the suffering. His goal is to obscure the redeeming hand of God.

This process of writing our stories requires daily yielding to Holy Spirit, pressing in close to the comfort and shelter of His wings. Since we cannot undertake this process in our own strength, we have provided several strategies to help you find shelter in God's protection as you write your story. Let's consider our Position, our Ponderings, and our Prayers.

Position Yourself Close to God

Stay close to God. Intimacy with the Father is the best shield against the enemy that we have. One of the major barriers between us and God is our relationships with other people. If we close our hearts to others, we close our hearts to God (Matthew 25:40-46).

> "Whoever claims to love God yet hates a brother or sister is a liar. For whoever does not love their brother and sister, whom they have seen, cannot love God, whom they have not seen." I John 4:20 (NIV)

As John Bevere teaches, harboring offense in our hearts against a brother or sister is the "Bait of Satan." When we allow unforgiveness or bitterness to grow in our hearts against another, we are drawn away from the shelter of God's wings. Ask God to help you keep your heart open to others; however, use discernment if you are in a relationship characterized by dishonor or manipulation -- get help to be safe. Offense is usually disguised in our hearts, so we need God to search us and reveal any bitterness that has come between us and others. (*Psalm 139:23*) Healthy boundaries are vital, but bitterness is not.

> "If you say, 'The Lord is my refuge,' and you make the Most High your dwelling, no harm will overtake you, no disaster will come near your tent. . . .
> 'Because he loves me,' says the Lord, 'I will rescue him;
> I will protect him, for he acknowledges my name.
> He will call on me, and I will answer him; I will be with him in trouble,
> I will deliver him and honor him.' " Psalm 91: 9-10, 14-15 (NIV)

When God shows us how we have distanced ourselves from Him by holding offense against others, we repent and give the situation into God's care which opens our heart once again. An open heart enables us to hear God's voice more clearly.

Use this prayer from our ENGAGE Prayer Method if it rings true for you:

> "God, I invite you to search me and reveal my deepest thoughts. Although you are acquainted with my heart and what I harbor, I am tempted to hide. Without your help, I do not know my own heart. Examine me and let me know what you find in my deepest thoughts. You do not condemn me. No, you love me and want me to be free. Help me accept what you see in my unveiled heart. I do not want to hide from you. I desire to open my heart to your bold love that I may know the joy of your presence."

Tune into Your Ponderings

As you engage in the process of writing your story, pay attention to your ponderings. What are you thinking about? Is your heart heavy or hopeful? Satan is the Accuser. He desires to fill your thoughts with lies about who you are and who God is.

> *"Fill your mind with that which is true, noble, right, pure, lovely. If there be any virtue, and if there be any praise, think on these things. Fill your mind and heart with things to praise, not things to curse." Philippians 4:8 (NIV)*

Ask God to help you be aware of your thoughts. Allow Holy Spirit to quicken your mind and heart to notice when you are assailed by lies.

Our mind is a battle ground. As soon as we quiet ourselves to focus on God, we are besieged by swirling thoughts. It is not surprising that this happens: the last thing Satan wants is for us to settle in for a rich conversation with our Father. Knowing that the battle is real, we invite God to take every thought captive, to settle our minds by inviting clarity and focus. (*2 Corinthians 10:5*) We ask the Lord to remove confusion, distraction, or double-mindedness from us.

Use this prayer from our ENGAGE Prayer Method if it rings true for you:

> "Father, you created my mind and called it good. At times, I feel that my thoughts betray me, but I know you can help me focus and take every thought captive. I repent for my pride and rebellion that fight against you. I long to be submitted to you completely, to be obedient to you even in my thoughts, Jesus. I place myself in your capable hands and invite you to be Lord over my mind."

One of our favorite declarations to renew your mind is *The Father's Love Letter* which you can find at http://www.fathersloveletter.com/.

If you are burdened as you reflect on your life, realizing how your story has been wrecked by pain, know that there is nothing too broken or too dark for Jesus to repair. Absolutely nothing is out of reach of God's healing mercies. You may want to "soak in God's presence" as you listen to this song, "The Harlot" by Misty Edwards:
https://www.youtube.com/watch?v=oydZCviFwzs

Seek Perseverance in Prayer

Staying connected with God through prayer is not just a good idea -- it is a necessity. Remember that prayer is not only talking to God, but also listening. Keeping the prayer channels open enables you to receive messages from Holy Spirit rather than from the Accuser. You can pray Scripture to build up your mind and heart with truth, such as:

> "God can do anything, you know-- far more than you could ever imagine or guess or request in your wildest dreams! He does it not by pushing us around but by working within us, his Spirit deeply and gently within us."
> Ephesians 3:20 (The Message)

Use this Scripture-paraphrased declaration as a blessing for your identity in Christ:

> "You are beautiful and you are beloved. God has blessed you with His love. God smiled on the day He created you. . . . Your world needs you. You bring something to your family that no other person has. They need the gifts you bring. Your family would not be complete without you. Others in your circle need the deposit that God has placed in your life." (Sylvia Gunter and Arthur Burk, *Blessing Your Spirit*, p. 2)

God loves to receive our prayers and declarations. He also desires to speak. God asks us to pay attention, to be silent and give Him a chance to reply. (*Job 33:31*) He desires to answer our questions. This prayer from the ENGAGE Prayer Method can help to strengthen your spirit:

> "I am expectant at how you are going to speak to me, Father. I hope to experience a new way of hearing your voice and recognizing your fingerprints. Help me to reject the Accuser's condemnation that weighs me down with despair and doubt. Thank you, Father, for drawing near to me and whispering your mysteries into my mind and heart."

As you consider your Position, Ponderings, and Prayer, we bless you to invite God to be your strength. Exodus 14:14 promises, *"The LORD will fight for you; you need only to be still." (NIV)*

You do your part to position yourself under the shelter of God's wings, taking every thought captive through prayer, but ultimately, God is the One who acts on your behalf.

Fuel Your Determination

The writing process may be profoundly challenging. Although difficulties are unpleasant, the psalmist highlights the value of persevering through pain: *"It is good for me that I was afflicted, that I might learn your statutes." Psalm 119:71 (ESV)*

When God calls us to write our stories, we respond with hope. It is discomforting to discover that there may be an element of frustration, despair, or hopelessness in the challenge. I have to admit that as I yield to God, I am motivated by a desire to learn to walk in His ways so that I can acquire His blessing and protection. The verses that talk about finding life through death and growth through affliction are not my favorites. **And yet, it appears God is more interested in your heart and your growth than in your ease.**

For some reason, growth is rarely achieved without some measure of discomfort or even outright pain. Think of a baby's birth, cutting teeth, learning to walk, limbs that ache during a growth spurt. God knows that this is the case, and He has provided relief in His Word: *"This is my comfort in my affliction, that your promise gives me life." Psalm 119:50 (ESV)*

Alright, we must admit that pain is part of growth. So if affliction is coming, how do we endure these times of trial and valleys of despair? To put it in perspective, let us consider Job, the righteous man from Uz. When Job suffers unimaginable loss, he refuses to curse God and die, although this might have been a tempting offer. How does Job remain steadfast? How does he persevere in the face of anguish?

Job treasures God, and he is treasured by God. His life is sustained by his heart for the Lord: *"For where your treasure is, there your heart will be also." Matthew 6:21 (NIV)*

When everything else falls apart, and destruction is loosed in his life, Job discovers that there is an unshakable foundation beneath his feet: the Rock of his salvation. Satan has no clue when he attempts to wreck this man's life, that Job has an inner strength that will never be broken. Despite mounting afflictions, Job slowly apprehends that he has a fire in the pit of his belly that will not be quenched by any suffering that the enemy launches against him. **In fact, his determination is galvanized by affliction.**

Job proves that the Word is his treasure, just like the psalmist professes: *"Your word I have hidden in my heart, that I might not sin against you." Psalm 119:11 (NIV)*

We bless you with a steadfast spirit as you persevere in the writing of your devotional. May your determination be fueled by God's strength which is sufficient for the task at hand. *You can do it, Baby!*

Prepare Your Personal Battle Plan

We have included practical tips for your Spiritual Battle Plan by detailing ways that we seek peace during the storm. God renews and strengthens us in many ways – not solely through traditional "spiritual" practices. Refreshment and a change of routine can also work wonders. We bless you to experience Jesus as your Savior during this writing process in new and marvelous ways.

Now let's get your personal battle plan in place. We begin by prayerfully considering the following questions.

Step 1:

Record here the Declaration that you wrote on page 27 (DECLARE Stage 5).

Step 2:

What are the common "lies" that attack me regarding my identity, who I am as a person?

Find Scriptures that combat these lies.

List the lies and Bible references here.

Lies about my Identity	Scriptural Truth

Step 3:

What are the common "lies" that attack me regarding my story?

Find Scriptures that combat these lies.

List the lies and Bible references here.

Lies about my Story	Scriptural Truth

Step 4:

What are the common "lies" that attack me regarding my ability as a writer?

Find Scriptures that combat these lies.

List the lies and Bible references here.

Lies about my ability as a Writer	Scriptural Truth

NOTE: Make index cards or print pages with the verses written out that you can post in a prominent place. Or make a flip book with the verses where you can refer to when you need reinforcement of truth to combat the lies. This is part of your Personal Battle Plan.

Step 4:

Now consider practical steps that you can take to fight back when you are under attack. We have provided some ideas in the concept map below. Add to those ideas anything that you have found to work in the past. Write down at least three options for yourself.

Step 5:

Reflect on any other ways that you have felt attacked since beginning this project. Ask God, *"How can I respond from a place of strength in You? What can I do when these lies come after me?"*

The enemy has plans to take us down, but Christ has defeated him. When you prepare your Spiritual Battle Plan, you prepare yourself to find your shelter under the wings of the Almighty. Let us remember this bold promise found in Isaiah chapter 40:

> "He gives strength to the weary and increases the power of the weak. Even youths grow tired and weary, and young men stumble and fall; but those who hope in the Lord will renew their strength. They will soar on wings like eagles; they will run and not grow weary, they will walk and not be faint."
> Isaiah 40:29-31 (NIV)

The Hebrew word for *weary* means "physical fatigue from lack of bread." Consider the Lord's Prayer in Matthew chapter 6 where Jesus instructs us to pray for our daily bread. While this can be understood as literal bread, it is also a symbol of Divine Provision. God supplies the strength we need to live according to His will. He is our strength when we are weak. He is the only Savior worthy of our trust. May you press in close to His heartbeat for you as you reveal the power of your God Story.

Phase One: Idea

Welcome to Phase One

Welcome to **The Power of Story** Idea Phase.

What should I write? Moving into the Idea Phase, you further engage with God as you journal, reflect, and listen. You consider many stories that could be told as you explore different possibilities.

During Phase one, you will:

- Gather insights from Ephesians 2:10.
- Create a timeline for personal reflection.
- Brainstorm your story ideas.
- Create a Support Team.

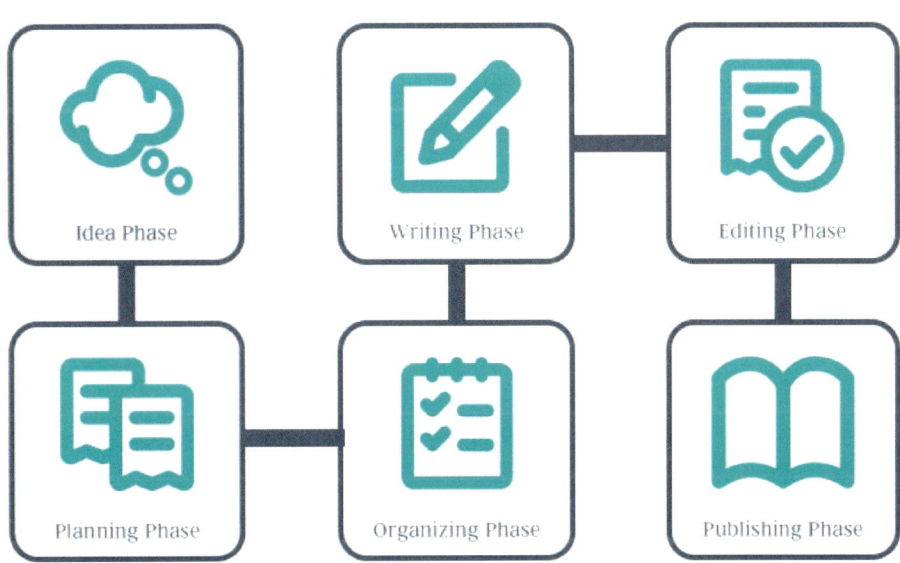

Phase One Checklist

Use this step-by-step checklist to complete the content for this phase. It will guide you as you navigate through the workbook and videos included in this phase of The Power of Story course.

- [ ] Watch the Video: The Devotional Writing Process and refer to Workbook Page 47.

- [ ] Watch the Video: Consider Your God Stories.

- [ ] Complete Workbook Pages 48-56.

- [ ] Watch the Video: Creating a Support & Prayer Team

- [ ] Complete Workbook Pages 57-58.

FLOURISH *Writers*
DEVOTIONAL WRITING PROCESS

IDEA PHASE
What should I write?
During this phase, you begin to prayerfully select which story to write?

PLANNING PHASE
What do I include?
During this phase, you will plan the elements of your story.

ORGANIZING PHASE
How do I prepare to write?
During this phase, you will organize the details of your story.

WRITING PHASE
How do I complete my first draft?
During this phase, you will learn the elements of a well-written story.

EDITING PHASE
How do I strengthen my writing?
During this phase, you will use our self-edit checklist to refine your story.

PUBLISHING PHASE
How can I share my story?
During this phase, you will be encouraged to share your story

Time of Reflection

Let us begin this week by reviewing our verse from Ephesians 2:10

"For we are God's handiwork, created in Christ Jesus to do good works, which God prepared in advance for us to do." (NIV)

Question 1
After meditating on Ephesians 2:10, what are my take-aways?

Question 2

If I am God's handiwork, or masterpiece, what does that say about the stories of my life?

Question 3

How has God prepared me in advance for taking this bold step to write my story?

My Personal Timeline

This is an exercise that invites you to reflect on your entire life up to now. You will create a timeline from birth to the present, listing as many major life-events as you can. You may want to also include favorite Scriptures that became meaningful to you during a season of life.

If you choose a horizontal layout, the events that you consider to be positive go above the line, and the events that you consider to be nega-tive go below the line. If you prefer a vertical layout, the events that you consider to be positive go to the right of the line, and the events that you consider to be negative go to the left of the line.

See the examples provided on the next page. You may want to work on another piece of paper first, and then copy your final version into this workbook. As you process your memories, there are some events that you forget the first time through, or you cannot remember the dates. This is a good opportunity to connect with others – reach out to friends or family from who may remember events or dates that you have forgotten.

Before you begin this exercise, we recommend that you prepare your heart to draw close to God with the Engage Prayer Method from the DECLARE Bible Study Approach: toss, catch, invite, open, and expect. Creating this timeline can be a bittersweet experience, and we want you to be supported by staying connected with Holy Spirit and resisting the voice of the accuser.

If you come under condemnation or become frustrated because you can't remember (or you remember too much!), use the Scripture verses included in the Engage process as declarations over your mind and heart.

My Personal Timeline

The ENGAGE Prayer Method

Toss
Throw your cares on God. Let Him bear your burdens.
Psalm 55:22

Catch
Receive the peace that surpasses all understanding.
Philippians 4:7

Invite
Take every thought captive. Invite clarity and focus.
Refuse confusion, distraction, or double-mindedness.
2 Corinthians 10:5

Open
Ask God if you have turned away or closed your heart to anyone.
**Release the offense, open your heart,
and give the situation into God's care.**
Psalm 139:23

Expect
Tell God that you are looking forward to hearing from Him. Let the excitement of time in His presence build expectation in your heart. Habakkuk 2:1

Use the space provided on the next page to record your personal timeline. Remember to keep it brief. Focus on the highlights.

My Personal Timeline

Brainstorm Story Ideas

Whew! Now that you have reflected on the seasons of your life and recorded the events on your personal timeline, you can step back and consider which story to write. As you engage with the following questions, we pray that you will perceive God's hopes and desires for you as you step out boldly to share the testimony of your life, a sacrifice of praise for His glory.

> *"The LORD your God has chosen you out of all the peoples on the face of the earth to be his people, his treasured possession." Deuteronomy 7:6 (NIV)*

Reflection 1
Does the thought of telling my story fill me with hope or fear, or perhaps a little bit of both? Process your reaction.

Reflection 2

Review the timeline that you created and prayerfully consider which stories from your life may need to be written, either to share with others or just for yourself. Write the top five possibilities.

Reflection 3

You may want to allow a few days to reflect on your possible stories. Or it may be immediately clear to you. After processing with the Lord, review Reflection 2 again and prayerfully consider the following question: *"Of all the stories that I could write, what story will I START with?"*

Reflection 4

Now think about any other people that may be involved in that story, and ask God to examine your ATTITUDE toward them. Is there any bitterness, offense, hurt, or resentment? Our written stories are for our personal healing until we are released by the Lord to share the details with others. Process these considerations with God in prayer.

Reflection 5

Write a PRAYER or a DECLARATION from your heart about your hopes for the process. If you identified any fears in **Reflection 1** above, ask God to give you a declaration of truth to combat those fears and doubts.

Create a Support Team

Writing a Spirit-inspired devotional is a sizeable undertaking, one that deserves support. The message God calls you to share is a powerful weapon against the forces of darkness. Because the enemy will do everything in his power to thwart you from fulfilling your call to write, we recommend that you gather a Support Team. Ecclesiastes 4:9 encourages us that "two people are better off than one, for they can help each other succeed." (NLT)

We recommend fulfilling three roles within your Support Team: Intercessor, Encourager, and Coach. If you struggle to find people who can provide these roles for you, do not fret. You have access to Holy Spirit who is more than able to provide all the support you need. If you cannot find anyone to commit to walking with you through this course, you have constant companionship and comfort with God himself.

You also have camaraderie with other FlourishWriters. Please reach out to us if you are faltering in any way. We want to know what difficulties you face. Your writing community is full of prayer warriors. You will find help if you seek it: *"Ask and it will be given to you; seek and you will find; knock and the door will be opened to you." Matthew 7:7 (NIV)*

Prayerfully consider who in your community can rally around you as you launch out in this writing project to provide intercession, encouragement, and coaching.

The Intercessor

- **Process** – pray as you process difficult memories and any other road blocks that try to get in the way.
- **Declare** – support you with Scripture to declare and pray during the planning and writing process.
- **Pray** – cover you in prayer every day, discern the strategy of the enemy.

The Encourager

- **Listen** – provide a safe place to share the trials and joys as you progress though the course.
- **Reflect** – help you remember where you have come from and where you are going, keeping the mission in mind.
- **Celebrate** – encouraging you to find joy in the process, celebrate each victory.

The Coach

- **Review** – provide a sounding board focused on the planning and writing process.
- **Critique** – offer feedback on writing decisions during the planning and drafting stages.
- **Edit** – offer their expertise by reading your first draft and providing a Friend Edit.

☐ Ask the Lord who can fulfill these support roles for you. Write several names of people who come to mind. One person may be able to perform all three roles, or you may have a different person for each one.

☐ Decide who you will invite to be part of your support team. If you cannot identify specific people, then ask God to bring someone across your path who can be a source of prayer support and encouragement to you. It may be someone you least expect. Keep seeking and you will find.

Approach people you have identified to request their support during this course. If you cannot find anyone specific who is willing to make that commitment, you can have a non-formal Support Team made up of special friends and family whom you call when you need any of the support that an intercessor, encourager, or coach provides.

Phase Two: Planning

Welcome to Phase Two

Welcome to **The Power of Story** Planning Phase.

What do I include in my story? During the Planning Phase, we zero in on the specific story that you are called to write. The step-by-step planning process guides you to summarize your story idea and reflect on your Key Scripture.

During Phase Two, you will:

- Choose the specific story you are called to write.
- Create a devotional map to plan your story idea.
- Study your Key Scripture.

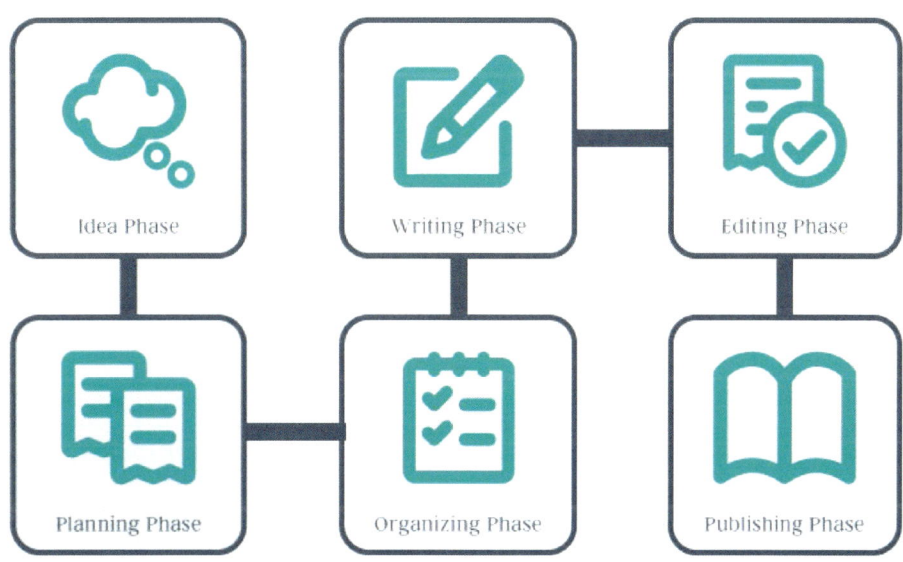

Phase Two Checklist

Use this step-by-step checklist to complete the content for this phase. It will guide you as you navigate through the workbook and videos included in this phase of The Power of Story course.

☐ Watch the Video: The Story Mapping Process.

☐ Complete Workbook pages 63-72.

☐ Review the Additional Resources on Pages 73-75.

Refine Your Story Idea

In the previous section, Decide Which Story to Write, you considered many personal devotional stories that you could write, and you selected one story as a starting place. With this story in mind, begin filling in the Story Map by writing the name of your story in the center oval. Answer the following questions to fill in the rest of the map. You can leave spaces blank, or you can add more spaces by hand if needed.

Reflection 1

What are the smaller Stories within the Story that I can tell? Write these on Story Map, or list here:

Reflection 2

Who are the People involved in this story? Write their names on the Story Map, or list here.

Reflection 3

What Places did this story take place? Write these on the Story Map, or list here.

Reflection 4

What are the Memories that come to mind? Write these on the Story Map, or list here.

Reflection 5

What are the Truths that I learned about myself and about God? Write on the Story Map, or list here:

Reflection 6

What are the Scriptures or Bible Stories that come to mind? Write these on the Story Map, or list here.

Choose Your Story

Now that you have created a Story Map, you can return to the Lord in prayer and consider the following reflections. These reflections are not presented in any particular order. You may feel compelled to start with a Scripture and consider which smaller story within the bigger story best represents that verse. Or you may start with a truth and decide which smaller story and Scripture best communicate that truth. Take time to listen and pray.

Reflection 1 – Smaller Story

What **smaller story** within the story excites me? What do I desire to write?

Reflection 2 - Truths
What compelling **truths** can be revealed within that smaller story?

Reflection 3 - Scriptures
What **Scriptures** may complement these truths within the smaller story?

Planning Your Story

Question 1
What is the story I wish to write? **SUMMARIZE** in one sentence.

Question 2
What is the **Key SCRIPTURE** that I want to use in this story?

Question 3

What is my **PURPOSE** in writing this story? What main message do I wish to convey?

Reflect on the Key Scripture

From our experience, spending time in God's Word fuels the writing process. We don't want to be like the Galatians who started in the spirit but continued in the flesh (Galatians 3). Let's keep our minds and hearts connected with Holy Spirit throughout the drafting process.

Using a journal or word processor, begin with the **Key Scripture** that you plan to use, and spend some time in Bible study. We recommend using an online resource such a Blue Letter Bible, Bible Hub, or Bible Gateway:

- Read the verse in several different translations.
- Read the whole chapter.
- What is happening in this book of the Bible? What is the context?
- Look up the cross-references for this verse.
- Read some commentaries, such as Spurgeon, Matthew Henry, or David Guzik.

What are some observations you made from your **Key Scripture?**

How do your insights relate to the story and purpose you wish to communicate? Summarize the Scriptural truths you would you like to communicate in your story.

Look back at "Planning Your Story," Question 3: What is my **PURPOSE** in writing this story? What main message do I wish to convey? Do you wish to revise or adjust this in any way?

Additional Resources

Devotional Idea & Planning Phase

What is the STORY I am writing?

Bigger Story: Personal Encounter with God

Smaller Story: What God taught me about walking by faith and not by sight.

What is my KEY SCRIPTURE? "So, we don't look at the troubles we can see now; rather, we fix our gaze on the things that cannot be seen. For the things we see now will soon be gone, but the things we cannot see will last forever" 2 Corinthians 4:18

Devotional Map

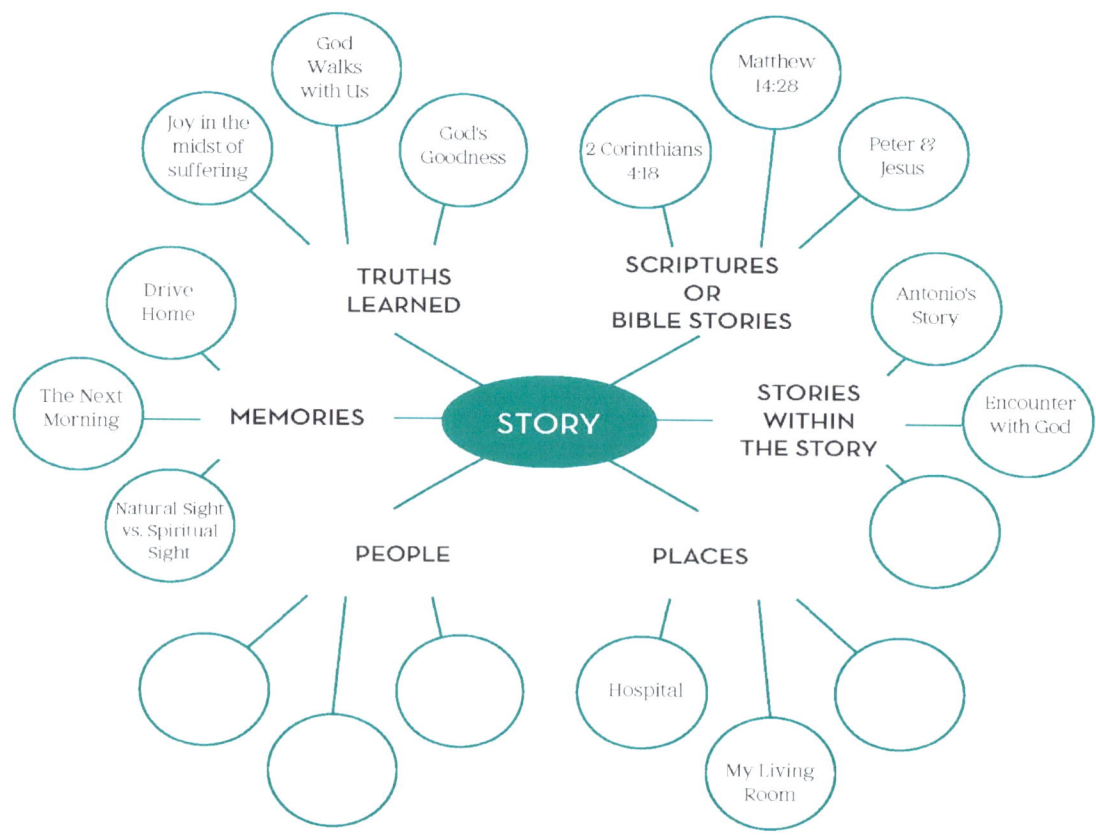

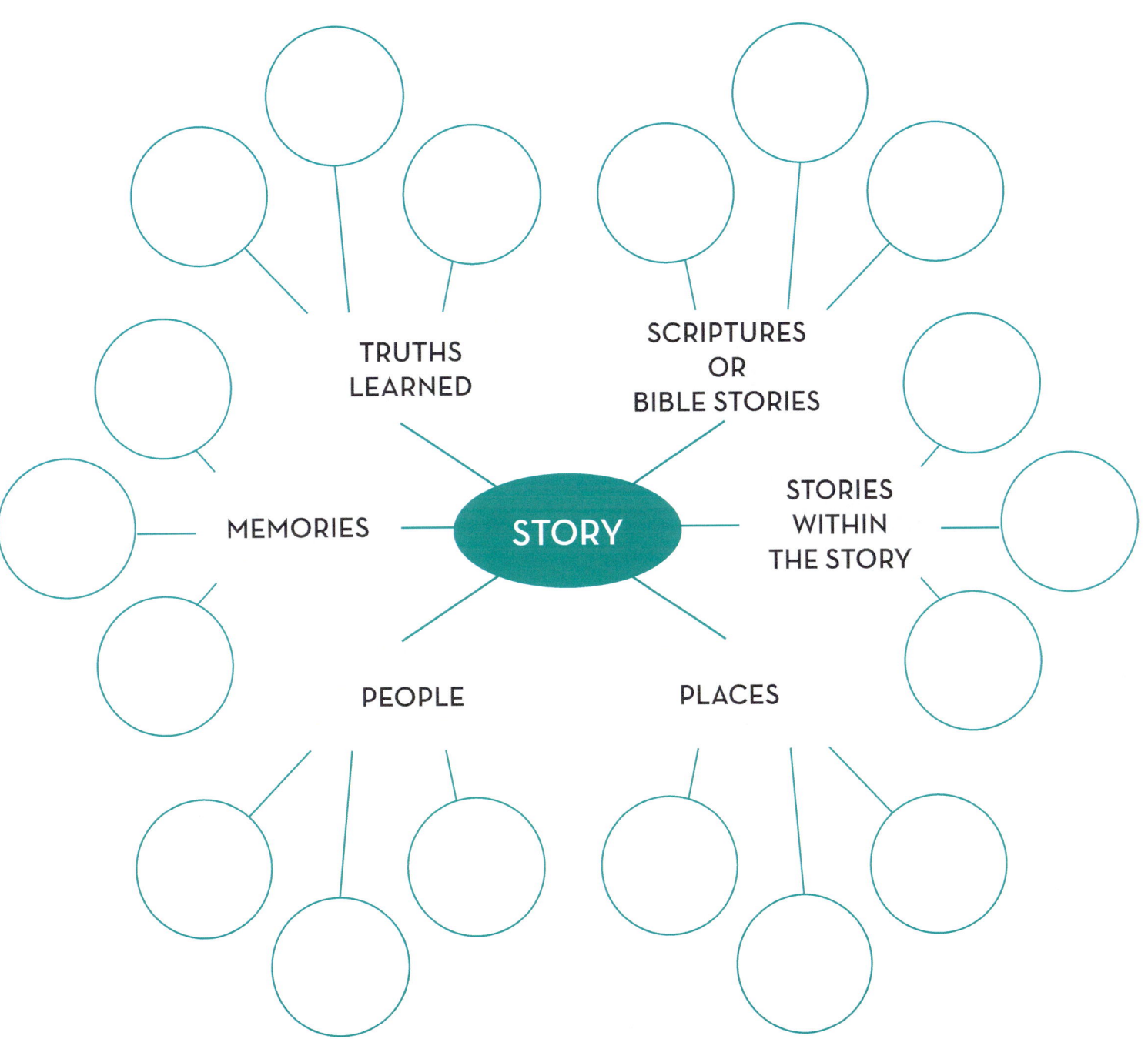

Phase Three: Organizing

Welcome to Phase Three

Welcome to **The Power of Story** Organizing Phase.

How do I prepare to write? Now that you have identified the specific story you're going to write, it's time to get organized. The organizing process guides you to clarify the purpose your story will communicate. The purpose is supported by your Key Scripture which anchors your story in God's Word.

In Phase Three, you will:

- Refine and summarize the details of your story.
- Write a Purpose Statement.
- Understand the needs of your reader.
- Prepare to write by creating a devotional outline.

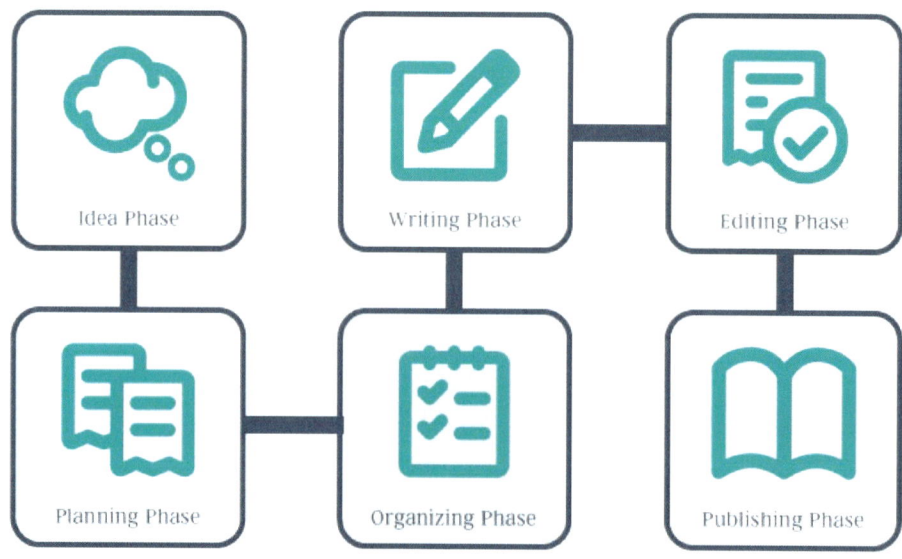

Phase Three Checklist

Use this step-by-step checklist to complete the content for this phase. It will guide you as you navigate through the workbook and videos included in this phase of The Power of Story course.

- [ ] Use Workbook Page 80 to make notes as you Watch the Video: What is a Purpose Statement?
- [ ] Use Workbook Page 81 to make notes as you Watch the Video: Clarifying Your Purpose.
- [ ] Use Workbook Page 82 to make notes as you Watch the Video: Communicating Your Purpose.
- [ ] Watch the Video: Organizing Your Story Details.
- [ ] Complete Workbook Pages 83-84.
- [ ] Review Additional Resources on Pages 85-86.

What is a Purpose Statement?

Watch Video and take notes here:

Clarifying Your Purpose

Watch Video and take notes here:

Communicating Your Purpose

Watch Video and take notes here:

Organizing Your Story Details

What are the details that I may want to include in this story? Brainstorm memories, people, and places.

Now imagine telling your story to another person. Missing anything? Go ahead and add in details until you feel that the story makes sense to you. Remember this is a smaller story within a larger story. You will not be able to say everything. Ask God to help you.

Think about how you will tell your story. Record the details here in a logical flow.

NOTE: If you are planning to share your devotional story with others, consider who your reader will be. What details would your reader find useful to grasp the message you wish to convey? Include those in the list above.

Additional Resources

Devotional Organizing Phase

What is my PURPOSE? When our focus shifts away from who God is, the problem captures our vision instead. Adrift on the tossing waves, we lose sight of His promises.

Devotional Details

- Antonio's Story
- The next morning
- Encounter with God
- Story of Peter walking on water
- What it means to "Walk by Faith"

Devotional Outline

- I was walking hand in hand alongside my dear friend who was losing her young three-year old son to a tragic brain injury.

- The next morning, I began processing the night before with God -- in my spirit I knew something was wrong within me. I had lost my focus, and I could see only sorrow.

- God continued to show me He was there all along. His promise had been fulfilled. He was our lifeline, our comforter through that tragic night.

- As I pondered the heartbreak of walking beside my friend, the story of Jesus and Peter walking on water came to mind.

- The only way we are going to see the hand of God guiding us through a raging storm, is to *fix our gaze* on His guiding hand.

Phase Four: Writing

Welcome to Phase Four

Welcome to **The Power of Story** Writing Phase.

How do I complete my first draft? With our planning and organizing process, you're fully prepared to get those words from your head onto paper. Even the most reluctant writer discovers that they are ready to write with the tools provided. The writing process is guided by examples from our own writing to demonstrate how to create a first draft.

During Phase Four you will:
- Practice the craft of a well-written story.
- Learn how to overcome writer's block.
- Discover the elements of the crucial first paragraph.
- Write your first draft.

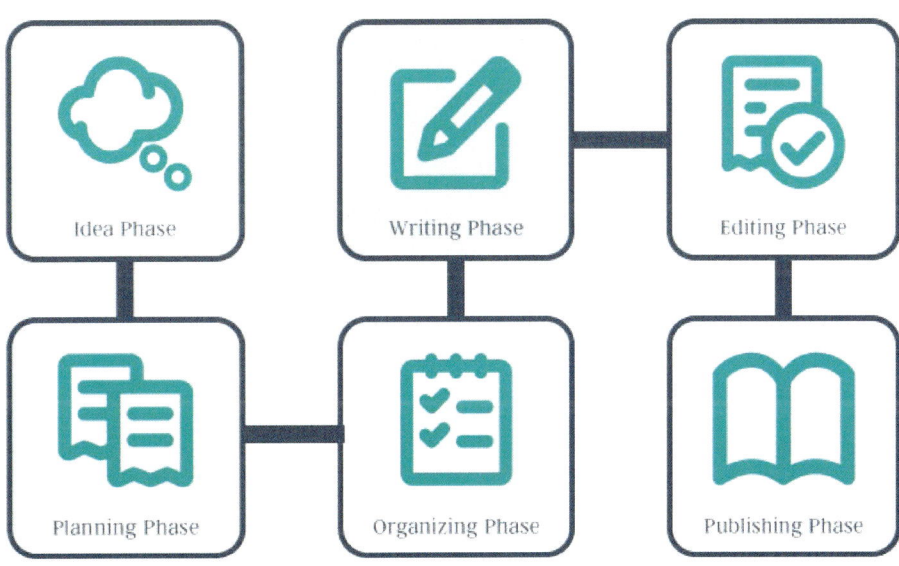

Phase Four Checklist

Use this step-by-step checklist to complete the content for this phase. It will guide you as you navigate through the workbook and videos included in this phase of The Power of Story course.

- [ ] Watch the Video: The Art of Storytelling and reference Workbook Pages 91-93.
- [ ] Watch the Video: Tips for Writing Your First Draft and reference Workbook Page 94.
- [ ] Use Workbook Page 95 to make notes as you Watch the Video: The Crucial First Paragraph Part I
- [ ] Use Workbook Page 96 to make notes as you Watch the Video: The Crucial First Paragraph Part II
- [ ] Use Workbook Page 97 to make notes as you Watch the Video: The Crucial First Paragraph Part III
- [ ] Review Scriptures to Keep Your Writing on Page 98 and begin your First Draft!

The Art of Storytelling

Tips for Writing a Well Written Story

Tip 1	A well written story immediately draws the reader into the scene.
Tip 2	A well written story has a powerful hook in the beginning paragraph.
Tip 3	A well written story helps you feel the tension through the details given about the people and situations involved.
Tip 4	A well written story has a careful amount of descriptive details, but not so many that they become a distraction.
Tip 5	A well written story shows vulnerability and admits mistakes.
Tip 6	A well written story has easy flowing transitions.
Tip 7	A well written story doesn't leave the reader in the mess too long but pulls them out with a glimmer of hope.
Tip 8	A well written story lets you know there is a battle for the soul taking place, but God's power is beginning to emerge.
Tip 9	A well written story shows us that nothing is impossible with God and His love trumps all.
Tip 10	A well written story makes the reader excited about finding joy and restoration from God in their own lives, while recognizing it will take time, effort and perseverance.

Acknowledgement: Many thanks to Tracie Miles of Compel for creating this tip sheet.

A Heart of Abundance

Tips for Writing a Well Written Story Devotional Example

". . . Out of the abundance of the heart his mouth speaks."

Luke 6:45 (ESV)

==What spills out of your mouth when you are squeezed?== **TIP #2**

> When my then-unchurched boyfriend (now-believing husband) accompanied us for the first time on a family road trip, we experienced an amusing incident that exposed a clash of cultures. Nearing home in the dark of night, we ran over a sizeable obstacle in the road which tore through our oil pan and brought our vehicle to a screeching halt. The shock of the incident elicited exclamations from everyone in the vehicle.
>
> "Help us, Jesus!" screamed Mom.
>
> "Praise God!" yelled Dad.
>
> "$#*@!!!" bellowed my boyfriend. **TIP #1 & 4**

==And then there was silence. The expletive hung in the air, a strange sound in our ears.== **TIP #3**

==Four years later, I married that young man, and I have imagined myself superior to him because I do not swear in anger.== **TIP # 6**

==I believed that this verbal self-control put me a step above my spouse on the "righteousness meter."== **TIP # 5** One day during an argument with my husband, I trotted out this fact as evidence of my superiority (you can imagine how that went over) to which he replied,

"I may curse in the more obvious fashion, but your cursing is just as cutting, perhaps even more so, cloaked in disdain, mocking, and shaming arrogance."

==Ouch! You know that feeling when a truth bomb has detonated, but you absolutely do not want to admit it?== **TIP #5**

==Jesus delivers a similar rebuke in Matthew chapter 5 when he tells us that our human "righteousness meter" is not as accurately calibrated as we imagine.== **TIP #6**

Jesus exposes a fundamentally human weakness: we wish to calibrate our sense of righteousness by comparing ourselves with others rather than with Christ. Unfortunately, this human-to-human comparison leads to deception not to discernment. (2 Corinthians 10:12-18)

None of us is good enough. Spiteful attitudes, thoughts, and words spring up unbidden from the self-centered nature of every human being. Certainly, we desire to place our hope in God, but there is a war going on inside us. Paul gives us insight into this battle with a personal revelation, *"I do not understand what I do. For what I want to do I do not do, but what I hate I do." (Romans 7:15, ESV)* **TIP # 8**

In Matthew chapter 4, we witness Christ speaking from a heart of abundance. We enter the story just after Jesus is baptized by John when He is *"led by the Spirit into the wilderness to be tempted by the devil." (Matthew 4:2, NIV)*

Do you notice the similarity to the story of Job? God allows the devil to test Job (Job 1:12). He also permits the devil to test Jesus. Here we get a chance to see how Jesus responds to an attack of evil designed to take Him down:

After fasting forty days and forty nights, he [Jesus] was hungry. The tempter came to him and said, "If you are the Son of God, tell these stones to become bread." Jesus answered, "It is written: 'Man shall not live on bread alone, but on every word that comes from the mouth of God.' " (Matthew 4:2-4)

Friends, do you see what just happened?! When Jesus encounters evil, He does not fight the attack with the power of his own qualifications, even though he could (He is God, after all). Instead, **Jesus confesses the Word.** *Selah — pause and think of this.* **TIP # 8**

When Jesus is squeezed, the abundance of His heart is God's Word. Here in Matthew 4 He is referencing Deuteronomy 8 in which Moses encourages the Israelite's to remember what God has done for them so that they trust in Him no matter the trials they face as they prepare to enter the Promised Land. **TIP #9**

I pray that you allow God to examine the abundance of your heart and reveal the thoughts and intentions that reside there. Allow Him to disclose your treasures, both lovey and not-so-lovely. He already knows your deepest thoughts, and He appreciates when you are honest with Him.

> God wants to celebrate with you and bring freedom where you are bound. Use the Scriptures, just like Jesus did, to protect you from the lies of the enemy. When you are full of God's truth, and life's troubles squeeze you, wisdom will come bursting out. Holy Spirit will inspire the Word hidden in your heart to guide you and to protect you. **TIP #10**

Tips for Writing Your First Draft

Open your journal or a new document on your computer. Start by writing three items from **"Planning Your Story:"**

1) Write the sentence that **SUMMARIZES** your story.
2) Write your **KEY** Scripture.
3) Write your **PURPOSE** Statement.

Our personal tips to remember when writing your first draft:

- Just write. Do not edit. You will edit later.
- Grammar, punctuation, and spelling do NOT matter. Later, yes, but not now.
- Remember that you are following a call, and God is your strength.
- Guard against the comparison trap. Your story has value because it has been purchased by Jesus' redemption. He is thrilled that you want to share your story as His story.
- If you get confused or lost, go back to **ORGANIZE YOUR STORY** and choose one of those details to explain. Write one or two sentences about it.
- If you can't think of what to write next, simply type or write, "Thank you, Holy Spirit, for leading me. Please give me what you want me to say." Thoughts will come. Write them down whatever they are.
- When you are stuck for the next sentence, it can help to speak out loud what you're trying to express and then write it. Tell the story to the mirror or to a friend.
- Do not listen to any inner voices that tell you "this is a bunch of junk." It's not. You are saying "Yes" to the call to write your story. You are bold and courageous.
- Speak out the **PRAYER** or **DECLARATION** that you wrote in Week Two.
- PRAY! SING! DANCE! Call a friend for prayer support!

The Crucial First Paragraph Part I

Watch Video and take notes here:

The Crucial First Paragraph Part II

Watch Video and take notes here:

The Crucial First Paragraph Part III

Watch Video and take notes here:

Scriptures to Keep You Writing

When you feel discouraged or stuck in your writing, spend some time declaring the Scriptures below.

1 Corinthians 2:16 – "I have the mind of Christ."

Matthew 19:26 – "With man this is impossible, but with God all things are possible."

Psalm 18:6 – "In my distress I called to the LORD; I cried to my God for help. From his temple he heard my voice; my cry came before him, into his ears."

Isaiah 49:23 – "Those who hope in me will not be disappointed."

I John 5:13 – "I write these things to you who believe in the name of the Son of God so that you may know that you have eternal life."

Hebrews 4:12 – "The word of God is alive and active."

Galatians 6:9 – "Let us not become weary in doing good, for at the proper time we will reap a harvest if we do not give up."

Phase Five: Editing

Welcome to Phase Five

Welcome to **The Power of Story**, Editing Phase.

Now that you have a first draft, it's time to get down to the nitty gritty of editing and revision. We want to help you to tighten the prose so that your story can clearly reveal God's glory. Don't worry, this is going to be more satisfying than you ever imagined. You will invite a friend to help, and the handy Self-Edit checklist guides you to overcome the most common pitfalls of devotional writers.

In phase five, you will:

- Learn an organized approach to edit and revise the content of your rough draft.
- Engage with your support team for a Friend Edit.
- Use the Self-Edit checklist to revise your devotional.
- Learn how to polish your writing and choose a title.

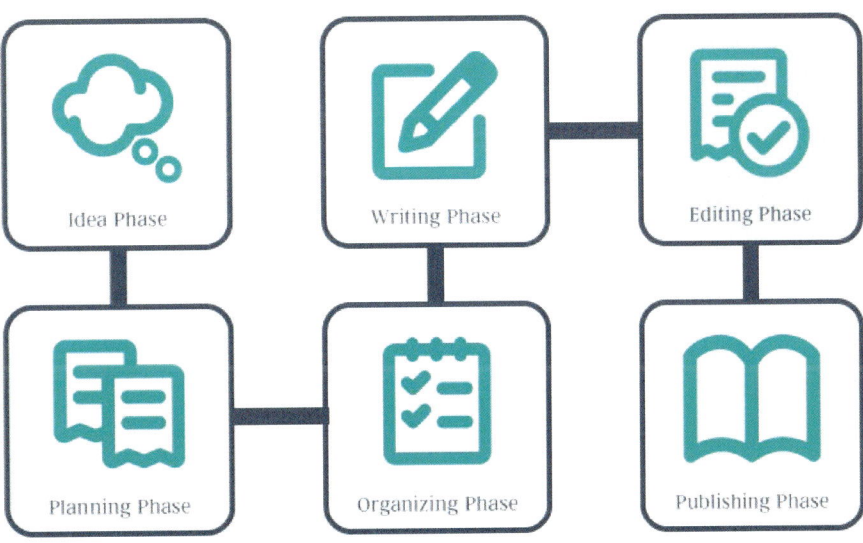

Phase Five Checklist

Use this step-by-step checklist to complete the content for this phase. It will guide you as you navigate through the workbook and videos included in this phase of The Power of Story course.

- [ ] Watch the Video: Introduction to the Editing Phase and refer to Workbook Pages 103-104.
- [ ] Watch the Video: Friend Edit and refer to Workbook Page 105.
- [ ] Review Workbook Pages 106-109 and Watch the Video: Self-Edit Checklist Example 1.
- [ ] Watch the Video: Self-Edit Checklist Example 2.
- [ ] Read Step 5: Create a Title on Workbook Page 110.
- [ ] Read The Final Draft in Workbook Page 111.
- [ ] Review Additional Resources on Workbook Pages 112-119. This "Devotional Writing Example" helps you to see how to write a first draft, receive a friend edit, and revise to create a final draft.

Overview of the Editing Process

Congratulations! You have a first draft of your God Story. Thank you, Lord.

Now we begin the process of editing your rough draft. You're nearly there. It requires training and perseverance to work up your writing muscles. Regardless of your experience, everyone benefits by taking a break between writing the first draft and editing. If you can put the piece away for a couple days before you begin editing and revision, you'll see it with new eyes.

Edit and Revise

When you have completed your rough draft and set it aside for a day or two, you are ready to edit and revise. This module guides you through these steps:

1. Check grammar and punctuation with a good word processor and Grammarly.

2. Read your draft aloud and revise anything that is unclear.

3. Friend Edit: Have someone in your support team read your draft using the checklist provided. Revise your draft.

4. Self Edit: Use the checklist for one last set of edits to your draft. Make final revisions to your devotional.

5. Create a Title for your devotional.

6. The Final Draft is complete!

Steps 1 & 2

Step One: Check Grammar and Punctuation

With a good word processor and Grammarly, you don't need to be a grammar or punctuation expert. These programs do not pick up every issue, but they do catch many common errors.

We use Microsoft Word which flags problems in the text, such as subject-verb agreement, capitalization errors, and wordy phrases. If you are unfamiliar with this feature, you can find out more at www.support.office.com

Follow the directions at www.grammarly.com to learn how to use the free grammar checking tool to review your rough draft. Grammarly keeps track of your common errors over time and gives you a report on how you're doing.

Step Two: Read Aloud

Print out your draft and read it aloud. The process of speaking and hearing the words highlights awkward phrases. It simulates what will happen in the reader's mind when they read your words. Have a highlighter handy to mark any rough patches.

This technique draws your attention to words and sentences that are in the way. When you lose interest in a part of the story, or find yourself tongue-tied, these are clues that you need to revise that section.

When you complete this process once and revised the piece, you can do it again a second time, but now record yourself reading your devotional. We use a digital recorder on our phone. As you listen to your words, grab your highlighter again and make note of any awkward or confusing sections. Revise again. Now you're ready to get input from a friend.

Step 3: Friend Edit

It is time to ask a friend or family member to look at your rough draft. Be sure to include your **Summary** sentence, **Key Scripture**, and **Purpose Statement** so that you and your reviewer can refer to them.

Ask your friend or family member to read your piece and use this checklist to provide feedback:

- ☐ *Did you stumble over any words or sentences?*
- ☐ *What didn't sound right, or what did you have to read again to make sense?*
- ☐ *Did the story present anything that was not explained? Were there any confusing parts?*
- ☐ *Did my writing invite you to encounter God and receive an inspiring message of hope?*
- ☐ *What is the strongest aspect of the story?*
- ☐ *What is the weakest part of the story?*

Feedback can be both discouraging and encouraging. You have poured your heart into this draft, and negative comments can be hard to hear. Prepare yourself with prayer before you review your draft with another, and make sure you choose someone who honors and supports you.

Revise your draft using the feedback from your Friend Edit. We recommend that you keep several drafts of your story. You may make changes that you regret and wish to recall how you expressed something originally. Once you have completed your revisions, take a little break before you embark on your Self Edit.

Step 4: Self Edit Checklist

Ready to tackle the finishing touches? Here are the four topics within the Self Edit:

- **Crucial First Paragraph**: *Did I include an interesting hook?*
- **Purpose**: *Does the story communicate the message I intended?*
- **Continuity**: *Does each paragraph move toward the purpose?*
- **Polish Your Writing**: *What can I delete or revise?*

☐ Crucial First Paragraph: Did I include an interesting hook?

Check your opening paragraph or series of sentences. Do you invite the reader into an interesting scene? You don't want to open with words or thoughts that are too shocking or overwhelming, but rather curious or intriguing.

The crucial first paragraph welcomes your reader into the story and hints at the message they will discover if they keep reading. If you are sharing a difficult story, it is important to allude to the glimmer of hope to come.

Are you satisfied with what you have? Do you want to make any changes here?

☐ Purpose: Does the story communicate the message I intended?

We write stories to testify to the power of God in our lives. We want the message that is burning in our hearts to make an impact in the lives of our readers. Most of us start off writing self-centered stories, but the more we write to share a larger message, we learn to craft God-centered stories. This awareness takes time and comes with practice.

In your devotional writing, you want to move beyond writing a laborious (some might say *boring*) chronological account of your life events. Instead, you desire to weave a narrative that invites the reader to encounter God and discover the inspiring message that you are called to communicate through your writing.

Check your devotional for the following:

- ☐ Did I address the reader by saying "you" or "friend" (or something like that) in my devotional?
- ☐ Where can I pose a question to help the reader think about how this message applies to their own life?
- ☐ Can I point to one or two strong sentences that communicate the purpose I hope the reader takes away? If not, add these sentences, especially at the end of the piece.

☐ Continuity: Does each paragraph move toward the purpose?

Read each paragraph, one at a time. Stop at the end of each one and ask yourself, "Did this paragraph take the reader one step closer to the message that I want to communicate? Did it support the overall purpose in this devotional, or did it take us off track?"

Be strong and brave: remove any bunny trails. We must be prepared to cut the fat from our first draft. Do not hold on tightly to your words. I make another file of "scrap" text that I can use for other stories. It helps me to *cut and paste* rather than *delete* since I feel like I did not write the words in vain. And indeed, those scraps do come in handy as content for other devotionals.

This is a good time to check the **length of your sentences and paragraphs**. The modern reader is less inclined to read long portions of text. It is helpful to break up the heaviness of your text with shorter paragraphs (2-4 sentences) or even a single stand-alone sentence. We mentioned in the point above posing a question to the reader. That question can stand alone as a bridge between two paragraphs.

☐ Polish Your Writing: What can I delete or revise?

Editors often cut 10-20% (or more!) from a rough draft. What remains is a more readable, lighter, leaner draft. How do they do this? One way is to remove extra words that take up space without adding value. You can use the *search and replace* function in your word processor to identify these words.

How do your sentences begin? Examine your sentence openers for unnecessary words. Eliminate filler phrases such as:

- ☐ *There is / There are / There were*
- ☐ *Due to the fact that*
- ☐ *The thing is / One of the things*
- ☐ *On the other hand*
- ☐ *Basically*
- ☐ *Just then*
- ☐ *I believe / I think*
- ☐ *In order to*

Overused words should be deleted. Your sentences will thank you. We are not 100% compliant at Flourish, but we are steadily improving:

- ☐ *About*
- ☐ *Actually*
- ☐ *Just / Just then*
- ☐ *Absolutely / Utterly*
- ☐ *Completely / Simply*
- ☐ *Rather*
- ☐ *Practically*
- ☐ *Somehow / Somewhat*
- ☐ *Thing*
- ☐ *A lot*
- ☐ *Extremely*
- ☐ *Kind of / Sort of*
- ☐ *Too*
- ☐ *Nearly*
- ☐ *Really*
- ☐ *Very*
- ☐ *Highly*
- ☐ *Totally*

Choose Wow! Words. Instead of attempting to strengthen your weak word with more weak words, choose a stronger Wow! word. Use an online thesaurus or the one in your word processor. Choose words carefully that fit your voice and style:

- ☐ *very, very* **pretty** ➔ *stunning, gorgeous, magnificent, splendid*
- ☐ *totally* **big** ➔ *substantial, enormous, weighty, formative, immense*
- ☐ *super-duper* **strong** ➔ *mighty, powerful, rugged, brawny, robust*
- ☐ *extremely* **smart** ➔ *brilliant, clever, bright, intelligent, brainy*

Replace worn out words. Adding *so* or *very* to these words does not make them more magical. Such words are dog-tired from overuse.

Use the blank spaces below to write down words you tend to overuse. Replace them with more imaginative selections. Try banning these words from your writing for a time. This restriction exercises your creative muscles and expands your vocabulary. As stated above, choose words carefully to match your voice and style. You do not need to show off your stunning vocabulary. Instead, create an enjoyable experience for your reader by selecting the right word:

- ☐ *so very* **beautiful** ➔ *attractive, delightful, ravishing, glamorous, exquisite*
- ☐ *so very* **excited** ➔ *overjoyed, enthused, ecstatic, thrilled, delighted*
- ☐ *so very* **fun** ➔ *enjoyable, amusing, pleasurable, entertaining, agreeable*
- ☐ *so very* **happy** ➔ *cheery, joyful, carefree, radiant, contented, satisfied*
- ☐ *so very* **sad** ➔ *sorrowful, dejected, depressed, miserable, mournful*
- ☐ *so very* **bad** ➔ *inferior, second-rate, inadequate, unacceptable, shoddy*
- ☐ *so very* **good*** ➔ *sound, robust, sturdy, strong, vigorous, superior*
- ☐ *so very* **nice** ➔ *pleasant, satisfying, marvelous, rewarding, inspiring*
- ☐ *so very* **interesting** ➔ *absorbing, fascinating, riveting, compelling, engaging*
- ☐ *so very* **amazing** ➔ *captivating, gripping, enthralling, glorious, enchanting*

- ☐ _____replace with ➔ _____

- ☐ _____replace with ➔ _____

- ☐ _____replace with ➔ _____

- ☐ _____replace with ➔ _____

* Except we do speak of God's goodness, and this is filled with potent meaning.

Step 5: Create a Title

The title is the first invitation to your reader and an indication of your purpose in writing this devotional. Depending on the intentions for this piece – whether you will share it with a larger group of people – the title may influence who will read your words.

Eight out of 10 people read headlines, but only two out of ten read the rest of the piece. Online readers are barraged by hundreds of choices daily. What will they choose to read? When you know, trust, and love the author, you will read what they offer, regardless of how the message is packaged. But if you meet a stranger, the odds of engagement are reduced. While there is no formula for writing a title, we do have a few tips to help you create one that works for you:

- At Flourish, we often create a title that comes from our Key Scripture or Purpose Statement. It's helpful when we can choose intriguing or slightly mysterious words.

- You can craft a strong title by using key words from the last sentence or paragraph of your devotional. This ensures two outcomes:

    1) Your devo clearly expresses the purpose with the main take-home message stated in both the title and the last sentence or paragraph.

    2) Your title gives a clear indication of the story's purpose. When the reader reads that last sentence or paragraph, they receive the warm glow of resonance and closure.

Have fun with it. One parting thought: clever is good, but confusing is not. You don't want a clever, confusing title. When you confuse, you lose. So make it straightforward, and if it is creative, all the better.

The Final Draft

Let's keep the editing and revision process in perspective. The beauty and power of your story is your testimony to God's faithfulness, and the hope that you offer to others. We pray that you do not become overwhelmed by the editing process. It is necessary to become a self-editor to some degree, but if this is your first attempt at writing, getting your story onto the page is a monumental accomplishment.

We suggest that you engage with the editing process to the extent that you are able. If it becomes overwhelming, take a break and come back to it when you are ready. If you're energized by it, keep going!

May you be encouraged by this observation:

> "Beautiful writing is merely the vehicle that conveys the story. By itself, language is an empty vessel. What gives language its life-changing power is the meaning it conveys, and that comes from one thing only: the story."
>
> Lisa Cron, *Wired for Story*

Yes! And a Holy Spirit Breathed God Story is best of all. We are delighted that you have chosen FlourishWriters to be part of your journey. We're cheering you on as you write your devotional. You have given substance to your testimony, enabling God's Word to become flesh for our generation. (John 1:14) We savor this gift and pray that God uses your story for the blessing of many.

Additional Resources

Devotional Writing Example

We have provided this example of a first draft, friend edit, and final draft of one of Jenny's devotionals.

First Draft

[Open with Personal Story]

"It's time Jenny, I have peace" my friend said over the phone. I could barely understand her as the words struggled to pass through her lips. Yet, ==I meticulously managed to string each syllable together, ever so painfully==, as the words made their full impact onto my heart.

Sometimes the sudden revelation ==we've just been hit with feels as if we have been left== stranded by God without a life preserver. We feel we are wading through a sea of despair, waiting for His promises to be fulfilled.

Have you been there?

I drove to the hospital knowing that the next several hours would be the most ==heart-wrenching, tragic, and emotionally exhausting== moment of my life as I walked hand in hand alongside a dear friend as she lost her young three-year old son to a tragic brain injury.

Watching a mother lose a child is not for the faint of heart. I drove home the night he passed away and my mouth could utter only one refrain through tear-stained sobs: *"OH, GOD, that was more painful than anyone should ever endure!"*

When I arrived home, I cried myself to sleep with the grief of the reality of the night pressed heavily upon my chest. The next morning, I began processing the night before with God, because in my spirit I knew something went wrong within me. I had lost my focus and I could only see sorrow.

I heard the Holy Spirit ask me, *"Jenny, what did you pray for?"*

"Father, I prayed for peace, and strength, your comforting presence, and something about it being beautiful in the midst of suffering...."

At that moment the Lord took me back to the night before, in my mind's eye, and said: "Didn't you *see* my strength in a mother holding her dying child? Didn't you *see* my peace poured out as everyone sang worship songs and praised My name?"

God would continue to show me He was there all along. His promise had in fact been fulfilled. He was our life-line, our comforter through that treacherous night.

This is what happens in the storms of life. The overwhelming reality of the natural shakes us and *we lose our focus and start staring at the problem, losing sight of the promise.*

[Pivot to Bible Story]

A favorite story to illustrate this point is the story of Jesus walking on water.

In Matthew 14:28 we come into the scene as Jesus is walking on the waters of the Sea of Galilee. Peter sees Jesus walking on the water and asks: *"Lord, is it you? Command me to come to you on the water."* (Matthew 14:28) Jesus beckons him out onto the water and all goes well for a few moments -- Peter is WALKING ON WATER! Until he sees the wind and begins to sink.

As soon as Peter saw the boisterous waves, he lost his focus, and he could not see the hand of Jesus reaching out to him. In the natural, walking on water is impossible because of something we call the law of gravity. It was only by the supernatural act of faith that he could do that. *Peter had to believe, he had to see that which cannot be seen....*

[Lessons from Bible Story]

We may not walk on water, but the only way we are going to see the hand of God guiding us through a chaotic world, through a chaotic storm is to *fix our gaze* on His guiding hand, to remain focused on His goodness, and to believe.

> *"So we don't look at the troubles we can see now; rather, we fix our gaze on the things that cannot be seen. For the things we see now will soon be gone, but the things we cannot see will last forever"* 2 Corinthians 4:18

The very eyes God gave us have the greatest ability to steal our faith by what we see. It happened to Peter on the water when he saw the boisterous waves, it happened to me in the hospital when I saw the reality of a tragic situation, it will happen to all of us.

[Application of Scriptural Truth]

So, if the ability of what we see can both rob us of our faith and build our faith, how do we remain confident in the promises of God? How do we fix our gaze on things that cannot be seen? *How do we experience joy in the midst of suffering?*

Just like Peter, as soon as we *see* those boisterous waves in our lives (because we will see them), we start asking God; *"God show me your hand!"*

As Peter cried out to Jesus — "Save me!" -- he saw the hand of Jesus! I believe the hand of Jesus was there all along because the Word assures us that God is continuously walking with us. So, when we start seeing those waves, we can confidently ask God to show us his hand in that situation. To remind us of the promise!

God is good, and He longs for us to see His glory, to perceive His outstretched hand among the chaos in our lives, in our families, in our hurting world.

==Joy springs from a place deep inside that believes in the promises of God==. If I want to experience an unshakable joy even in the midst of suffering, I must discover the kind of faith that is not built on the troubles I see around me, but rather what I know to be true about the goodness of God.

Ladies, our stories aren't easy, the roads we travel are often broken and our hearts long for the promise fulfilled in our lives. Yet, in the midst of the suffering, the waiting, the unknown, we must choose to see that which cannot be seen . . . *and we must choose to believe.*

Friend Edit Example

Friend Edit

- [ ] *Did you ==stumble== over any words or sentences?*

    Sentences can be tightened. The verbs are more complicated than they need to be, and descriptions are too wordy. Try developing the storm-tossed sea image a little more to show us how you felt.

- [ ] *What ==didn't sound right==, or what did you have to read again to make sense?*

    It's not confusing, but a little distracting when you change verb tenses from past to present

- *Did the story present anything that was not explained? Were there any <mark style="background-color: lightblue">confusing</mark> parts?*

    Don't assume that we know the point you're illustrating. Support the transition from the personal story to the Bible story.

- *Did my writing invite you to encounter God and receive an <mark style="background-color: pink">inspiring message of hope</mark>?*

    Yes! This is a difficult story to tell, but I was not in the mess too long before you point to the hope we have in Christ.

- *What is the strongest aspect of the story?*

    The Biblical truth is illustrated in the personal story. You share just enough detail to help me perceive the pain without becoming overwhelmed and having to disengage. You offer a fresh look at a well-known Bible story.

    I like how you engage the reader with a question early on. You may want to address the reader directly toward the end, asking them to look for God's hand in the difficult situation they face.

- *What is the weakest part of the story?*

    The heart of the message is well communicated, and this is the most important job of a writer. I sense your passion and Holy Spirit anointing to write. Tightening your language by cutting out extra words and keeping verb tenses consistent is an area of growth that will benefit your writing.

Final Draft Example

Choosing to See

"It's time Jenny. I have peace," my friend said over the phone. I could barely understand the words which struggled past her lips. Yet, I meticulously pieced together the halting syllables as her message collided into my heart.

She invited me to walk with her through a trauma too monstrous for either of us to bear. I felt tossed on a stormy sea, abandoned by God without a life preserver. Drowning in a sea of despair, I wondered how His promises of hope for the future could be fulfilled in the face of wounding so immense that it was bound to leave a scar.

Have you been there?

I drove to the hospital knowing that the next several hours would be the most heart-wrenching and emotionally exhausting time of my life. I was walking hand in hand alongside my dear friend who was losing her young three-year old son to a tragic brain injury.

Watching a mother lose a child is not for the faint of heart. I drove home the night he passed away and my mouth could utter only one refrain through tear-stained sobs: *"OH, GOD. This is more pain than anyone should ever endure!"*

When I arrived home, I cried myself to sleep with the grief of the night crushing my chest. The next morning, I began processing the night before with God -- in my spirit I knew something was wrong within me. I had lost my focus, and I could see only sorrow.

I sensed the Holy Spirit ask me, *"Jenny, what did you pray for?"*

After reflecting a moment, I replied, *"Father, I prayed for peace, and strength, your comforting presence, and that you would bring beauty in the midst of suffering."*

At that moment, the Lord took me back to the night before, in my mind's eye, and asked, *"Didn't you see my strength in a mother holding her dying child? Didn't you see my peace poured out as everyone sang worship songs and praised My name?"*

God continued to show me He was there all along. His promise had been fulfilled. He was our lifeline, our comforter through that tragic night.

Unfortunately, the darkness of the traumatic events blinded me to God's presence. The storms of life have a way of obscuring God from view. We know theoretically that He will never leave us nor forsake us, and yet, when tragedy strikes, we easily forget His promises.

As the raging winds and roaring waves loom large, our confidence in God diminishes. **When our focus shifts away from who God is, the problem captures our vision instead. Adrift on the tossing waves, we lose sight of His promises.**

As I pondered the heartbreak of walking beside my friend, the story of Jesus and Peter walking on water came to mind. In Matthew 14:28 we come into the scene as Jesus is walking on the waters of the Sea of Galilee.

Peter sees Jesus walking on the water and asks: *"Lord, is it you? Command me to come to you on the water."* (Matthew 14:28)

Jesus beckons him out onto the water and all goes well -- for a few moments, Peter is WALKING ON WATER! In the natural, walking on water is impossible because of the law of gravity. It is only by the supernatural act of faith that he performs this physically impossible act.

Peter can walk *on water because he believes. He sees that which cannot be seen.*

But when Peter's gaze shifts from his Messiah to the powerful storm, the sacred moment of faith ends and gives way to doubt. His confidence in Jesus is shaken by the physical impossibility of his condition, and he begins to sink. When Peter sees the boisterous waves, he loses his focus and no longer sees the hand of Jesus reaching out to him. Just like all who lose their lifeline to the Savior, Peter's faith withers, and he is overcome by the tumbling waves.

We may not experience the thrill of walking on water, nor the terror of sinking into the deep, but the only way we are going to see the hand of God guiding us through a raging storm, is to ***fix our gaze*** on His guiding hand. We stay afloat when we remain focused on His goodness, when we believe that He is able to overcome any obstacle.

> *"So we don't look at the troubles we can see now; rather, we fix our gaze on the things that cannot be seen. For the things we see now will soon be gone, but the things we cannot see will last forever." 2 Corinthians 4:18 (NLT)*

Although our eyesight is a wondrous blessing from God, it leads us astray when we focus on the storm that we can see instead of on the promises of God that last forever. Our sight builds our faith when we look for God's eternal purpose; however, our sight threatens our faith when we look at the circumstances.

Just like Peter on the water, terrified by his close-up view of the boisterous waves, and just like me in the hospital, grieved by the reality of my friend's suffering, doubt and fear press in on us, obscuring our view of the only One who can save us.

If what we see has the potential either to crush our faith or build our faith, how do we remain confident in the promises of God? How do we fix our gaze on things that cannot be seen? **How do we experience joy during suffering?**

Let us take a lesson from Peter's experience: as soon as you *see* those crushing waves in your life -- because you will see them -- start asking God, *"Please show me your hand!"*

When Peter cries out to Jesus – "Save me!" – he sees the hand of his Savior. I believe Jesus' hand was there all along because the Word assures us that God continually walks with us. So, when you see those waves, ask God to show you His hand in your situation, to remind you of His promises.

God is good, and He longs for you to see His glory, to perceive His outstretched hand in the chaos of this hurting world.

Joy springs from a place deep inside each one who believes in the promises of God. If we want to experience unshakable joy, even during suffering, we must cultivate an unwavering faith that regards the troubles we see in light of the steadfast goodness of God.

Ladies, this walk of faith is anything but easy. The roads we travel are broken, and our hearts long to see the promise fulfilled in our lives. Yet, even in the midst of the suffering, the waiting, the unknown, we must choose to see that which cannot be seen . . . *and we must choose to believe.*

Phase Six: Publishing

Publishing

You made it! Now you are ready to share your story with others. Please watch the Publishing Video. If you desire to have your draft reviewed by FlourishWriters, you may purchase a review, and then complete the pre-submission checklist below:

> [ ] *Complete the entire course, including the workbook and all training videos.*
>
> [ ] *Use Grammarly online to check and correct your grammar.*
>
> [ ] *Seek out a Friend Edit and follow the Self Edit checklist provided. Revise your draft as needed.*
>
> [ ] *Check that the word count of your piece does not exceed 1000 words. Most word processors will provide a word count for you.*

Once these steps are completed, please prepare the document as follows. You may use any word processor of your choice. Please save as a Word document, and format as follows:

> [ ] *Label the top of the document:*
>
> > *Title*
> >
> > *Your Name*
> >
> > *Word Count*
> >
> > *Story Summary Statement*
> >
> > *Key Scripture*
> >
> > *Purpose Statement*
> >
> > *Followed by the text you have written*

[ ] Save the file in this format:
  LastName, FirstName – FlourishWriters Review

[ ] To submit the devotional, please email as a Word attachment to

  info@flourishgathering.com

Once you submit your final draft you can expect:

[ ] to receive a confirmation email within 48-hours of submission.

[ ] to receive your devotional review feedback form as an attachment to an email within seven (7) days.

How do I share my story? We suggest that you seek the Lord for His ideas. When you make yourself available, you will notice open doors. God may send you a sister with a similar story who will be encouraged by your devotional. Perhaps you can seek out an opportunity to share your story at church or through another women's ministry. You may want to approach a blogger you follow to see if they would publish you as a guest writer. Or perhaps you blog yourself or are feeling the nudge to do so. Whatever path Jesus opens, we encourage you to step out boldly with your God Story. And let us know how it works out. We love to celebrate kingdom building, one story at a time.

> Forgetting what is behind and straining
> toward what is ahead,
> I press on toward the goal to win the prize
> for which God has called me heavenward in
> Christ Jesus.
>
> Philippians 3:13-14

Congratulations

We have come to the end of The Power of Story. However, we hope that this is just the beginning. The process of writing your first devotional – or at least your first FlourishWriters Devotional – ignites a desire for more.

We bless you to dream.

> *"God can do anything, you know - far more than you could ever imagine or guess or request in your wildest dreams!" Ephesians 3:20 (The Message)*

We bless you with confidence.

> *"Be strong and courageous. Do not be afraid; do not be discouraged, for the LORD your God will be with you wherever you go."*
> *Joshua 1:9 (NIV)*

We bless you to follow God's call on your life.

> *"My sheep listen to my voice; I know them, and they follow me."*
> *John 10:27 (NIV)*

We bless you to boldly share your God Stories.

> *"Now go; I will help you speak and will teach you what to say."*
> *Exodus 4:13 (NIV)*

We pray that this time with FlourishWriters releases you to write words for the glory of God. What an honor and privilege to join you in this journey.

Jenny & Mindy

Notes

Notes

Notes

Made in the USA
Middletown, DE
26 December 2018